YOU & YOUR CHILD
LEARNING
DIFFICULTIES

First published 1999

Letts Educational
Aldine House
Aldine Place
London W12 8AW
Telephone 020 8740 2266

Text: © BPP (Letts Educational) Ltd 1999

Author: Tony Eaude
Series editor: Roy Blatchford
Project manager: Alex Edmonds
Editorial assistance: Tanya Solomons

Design and illustrations: © BPP (Letts Educational) Ltd 1999
Design by Peter Laws
Illustrations by Madeleine Hardy
Cover design by Peter Laws

British Library Cataloguing in Publication Data
A CIP record for this book is available at the British Library.

ISBN 185758 9807

Colour Reproduction by PDQ Repro Limited, Bungay, Suffolk.
Printed and bound in Italy

Letts Educational is the trading name of BPP (Letts Educational) Ltd

Letts Educational would like to thank all the parents who sent in their tips for educating children
and who wrote with such enthusiasm about parenthood.

YOU & YOUR CHILD
LEARNING DIFFICULTIES

Tony Eaude

Contents

Words in **bold** are defined in the glossary at the back of this book.

"Do not confine your children to your own learning for they were born in different time."

HEBREW PROVERB

Dear Parent,

What happens at nursery and in primary school is vital to your child's education. What you do at home is just as important.

It's never too soon to start supporting your child's learning. The time that you spend with your child in the first months and years gives him or her a foundation that lasts a lifetime. Make the most of every opportunity for you and your child to enjoy learning together.

You don't need to be an expert. You do need to be enthusiastic – especially when you face the more difficult moments of bringing up a child. Remember that the time you invest at home will help your child achieve all through primary and secondary school and open up opportunities for him or her in the future.

This book is one in a major new series from Letts. It will help you support your child, with information about how to identify problems with a child's learning. It gives practical advice, and guidance on how parents, teachers and children can move forward together after identifying a particular learning difficulty.

The important thing is to make education fun – especially when your child is finding learning hard!

Roy Blatchford

ROY BLATCHFORD
Series editor

What do parents worry about?

What should I be worried about?

Most children make good progress and get on well at school most of the time. But many children – about one in five – need extra help at some time because they find learning difficult.

All parents worry about their children – it's natural. How children get on at school is one main source of worry – especially if your child is unhappy or has particular difficulties.

Some children's physical or mental disabilities mean that extra provision will always have to be made for them, sometimes at a **special school**. Most children carry on in mainstream schools with extra support. This book concentrates mainly on how children with learning difficulties can be identified and helped when they are in **mainstream schools**. If your child goes to a special school, you may need to seek further advice, perhaps using the organisations listed in the back of this book.

Learning problems

All sorts of things can affect how your child is learning. These may be related to:

- ✔ health
- ✔ behaviour
- ✔ concentration
- ✔ emotional upsets
- ✔ unidentified worries

Or your child may simply find learning difficult.

Parent quote

"I realise now that I pushed Martin too hard. I knew he was struggling, but I just couldn't bear the idea that he wasn't as 'bright' as his brother. In the end, my expectations probably made life much harder for him."

Schools identify children with learning difficulties as having special educational needs (**SEN**). This is not to label them, but to try to help, for instance by more support, specialist materials or extra reading. Teachers will usually have to plan even more carefully how to help your child, and should let you know what they are doing and how you can help. But you may find that you are upset, or you disagree, with the school's assessment or provision. Remember – you know your child very well and have a very important role in discussing and deciding what is best for him or her. If you work together with the teachers, you can really make a difference to your child's school life.

A child's view can easily get overlooked when important schooling decisions are being made. If your child is very young, or severely disabled, it may not be easy or possible to be sure what it is that they really want. Sometimes your child may want something impossible. But it is important to make sure that your child is involved in decisions if appropriate.

How you can help

You have to try to strike a balance, ensuring that you are:

✔ interested and supportive

✔ not overprotective or fussy

You may be able to help your child, for example with extra reading or a special way of managing behaviour. If you are overprotective, too pushy or too strict, you could make things worse.

Skills for life

Children with learning difficulties often need particular help to learn to:

✔ be independent and resilient
✔ stand up for themselves
✔ be confident
✔ try new things for themselves
✔ understand that adults are on their side

Give children responsibility and praise them when they show these qualities.

What if my child speaks a first language other than English?

If your child is learning **English as an additional language** that is not a reason in itself for him or her to be identified as having special educational needs. Of course, other reasons may make it appropriate. When young children – below about seven years old – are still in the early stages of learning English, it is very hard to assess whether there is a learning difficulty or whether progress in reading and writing is just delayed. Be careful –

schools do sometimes put young children on the **special needs register** when it isn't necessary. If this happens to your child, go and talk about it with the teachers.

What if my child is very able?

Most able children do well at school and do not find learning difficult. But it may be appropriate for schools to identify able pupils as having SEN – in particular when they need special provision because they are not being suitably challenged or are unhappy because of emotional or behaviour concerns related to their ability. This may require the advice of an **educational psychologist** or another specialist.

Talk about any concerns with professionals, like teachers and doctors. Don't keep worries to yourself. Talking with teachers (either at parents' evenings, or arranging a separate time) helps them and you. For instance, teachers need to know if your child has any health problems, like glue ear or short-sightedness, that can affect how your child learns. If your child finds it hard to concentrate or has tantrums, you and the school may need to work together to find out what is causing the problem. Often, if there has been a difficult time, such as parents separating or relatives being very ill, this will be one of the things that is affecting your child's progress.

Try to agree the best way to help and support your child by having high but realistic expectations and giving him or her the support needed. This will always involve what all children need – love, security and attention. At times during your child's schooling you may have to speak up and support him or her, especially if you think that the wrong decisions are being made.

> **Parent tips and quotes**
>
> "Find out as much as you can about any disability your child may have. The more information you have, the better you can cope with it."
>
> "We didn't know how well he was supposed to be getting on with his reading. But when the school fixed up extra help, he really caught up."
>
> "We had to battle to get any extra help at all – and even then we never felt it was enough."

Work with teachers whenever you can to get the best for your child.

What are special educational needs?

Schools use the term special educational needs (or SEN) for children who need extra help and support, sometimes permanently, sometimes to help through a difficult patch. About one in five children will be identified as having SEN at some time in their school lives.

> ### Parent tip
>
> "Don't let the bureaucracy get you down. Remember that it's your child's future you are deciding on. Make your voice heard."

There is a lot of confusing jargon, sometimes used differently by different people. You need to know some of it. The glossary at the back of this book explains the more common words. The main thing is: don't be afraid to ask if you don't understand something!

The Government's special needs **Code of Practice** says who has to do what. Usually schools and **Local Education Authorities (LEAs)** produce simple leaflets to help you, especially for specific physical disabilities. Organisations of parents and others give information or support. Some names are at the back of this book.

How do I know if the school thinks my child has special needs?

All schools keep a register of children identified as having SEN. You should be told when your child is on the register and at what stage. Do not be put off by the amount of paper you get. It is important that you put your views forward. Get someone – a friend, a **named person** or someone at the school – to help you if you want.

What are the stages?

There are five stages depending on the level of concern. Most children carry on in ordinary schools with extra support. In the first three stages, your child will nearly always remain in a mainstream school. After a set time (usually a few months) there is a **review** of progress to decide whether to keep your child at the same stage, or move him or her 'up' a stage if concerns are greater, or 'down' a stage or off the SEN register if things have improved.

STAGE 1:

The teacher has an initial concern and shares this with you, often at a parent-teacher discussion. The teacher will usually make suggestions about how you can help.

STAGE 2:

The teacher has more concern, and involves the school's **special needs co-ordinator (SENCO)**. He or she is a senior teacher who can advise you and keep a close track of progress when your child moves classes. The school should write down and discuss with you an **Individual Education Plan** (often shortened to **IEP**) to say what targets are being set for your child and the extra support put in to achieve these.

> **Parent quote**
>
> "I went in expecting the teachers and psychologist to be unapproachable and frightening, but they were really straightforward and caring. I definitely felt that they wanted the best for Paul too."

STAGE 3:

The concerns are considerable and outside advice or help is brought in. Almost always an educational psychologist will be involved, and possibly other professionals, such as doctors, speech therapists or specialist teachers. The school and you will receive written reports. The IEP will again outline targets and support, but will be more specific about the type of support and amount of time to be provided.

STAGE 4:

This is called a **multi-professional assessment (MPA)**. An officer from the LEA calls together the views of everyone (including you) involved with your child. This will always include the view of the educational psychologist and the school doctor. You can ask the LEA for an MPA if you feel that your child's needs are not being met at Stage 2 or 3. But discuss this closely with the school first.

STAGE 5:

The LEA then decides whether to issue a **statement**. If so, you will get a draft. Check to see that this includes specific provision of the necessary resources, such as equipment, extra teaching help and computers. You can challenge the draft statement or appeal if the LEA does not issue a statement. The school doctor makes an assessment before a statement is drawn up.

About 2% of all children have such severe needs that the LEA draws up a statement. The statement is a legal document which entitles your child to that support.

Parent quotes

"She needed a statement — they must have cut down hundreds of trees, the amount of paper they sent us."

"I was really scared when we had the first review, all those people there. But it showed that they really knew about my daughter's needs."

Stages 4 and 5 take quite a long time and involve a lot of paperwork. It may propose that your child goes to a special school or **special unit**. Say what you think, even if you think "I need more time to make a decision" or "I'm confused".

At all the stages there are regular reviews. With a statement this happens formally at least every year. Make sure you take part in the reviews.

This can seem very confusing and bureaucratic to parents. It is! But it does have a point – that your child gets the help and support that he or she needs.

How do I know if my child has learning difficulties?

Parents often find it hard to know what to expect of their children. It is hard to know whether your child has learning difficulties – and if he or she is experiencing problems how best to help.

When your child is a baby, doctors and nurses compare him or her to the average for other children of the same age. This works well for obvious things like weight and height. The same sort of idea is used for children's learning, but it doesn't work so easily because we all have different sorts of abilities which are not easily measured.

Identifying learning difficulties

The best advice on identifying learning difficulties and deciding what to do is to:

✔ watch how your child is getting on, especially over a period of time

✔ discuss your worries with other people to get a range of views

How much should I trust experts?

A word of warning

Agree with the teacher the best way to help your child. A lot of children get confused because they are being told to do things one way at home and another way at school. Children with learning difficulties benefit from a consistent approach, especially in reading and maths.

Experts have wide experience of learning difficulties and their causes, but children don't always behave as you expect when an expert sees them. Your judgement is vital too.

Discussions and reviews give everyone a chance to decide how concerned they are, what progress is being made and what to do next. You are important in all three parts, but remember that professionals do bring a wide knowledge of children as well as thorough training in their field of expertise. You probably know your child well, so make sure your observations and views are heard. However, you may not be very good at knowing how your child compares to other children or what action is needed. Be prepared to listen as well as give your opinion.

Usually, reviews with teachers result in specific individual targets being written down. This might be as clear as 'to learn the names of all the letters of the alphabet' or might refer to behaviour or attitudes that must be changed. You can play a big part in helping your child to meet these targets, partly by doing extra work with him or her, and partly by showing that you are working with the teachers and that you regard success as important.

Parent quote

"We were convinced that Susie wasn't progressing as fast as she should, but her teachers said that they were more than happy with her progress."

How useful are tests?

Tests only measure some parts of your child's abilities – mainly in using words, numbers and patterns. So treat them with caution. They do, however, give a good idea of how your child is getting on compared to other children and can often highlight areas to concentrate on.

SOME COMMON TESTS INCLUDE:

- When children start school, they do a **Baseline Assessment**. This gives an indication of how well a child is doing, especially in language development.

- When children are seven, and then again at 11, they do **National Tests** (formerly called Standard Attainment Tasks or SATs). These give an idea of how a child is doing in English, maths and science, compared to other children locally and nationally.

- During the year, schools often do reading or maths tests which may give a score compared to what other children of that age normally score.

But all of these tests are fairly general. Don't rely too much on them. If your child has learning difficulties, someone at school, maybe an educational psychologist, can use much more detailed tests to explore specific difficulties.

Parent quotes

"The best thing we ever did was to go and see the headteacher. She really got things moving."

"I didn't think to tell the school about his glue ear when he was three. But when he found it hard to get into reading, they thought that might have had something to do with it."

"After Tim's language skills were identified as being quite poor in his Baseline Assessment, both my wife and I spent more time on this area in his playtime and out of school activities. We saw quite a dramatic improvement in only a few months."

So what else can I do to help?

This varies enormously from child to child. In
general:
• If your child has a specific condition – especially a
medical one – find out about it and share that
knowledge with teachers. They will be grateful. Talk
to other parents whose children have had the same
experience. But be careful – this can result in you
becoming over-anxious or imagining the worst.

• Be prepared to speak up for your child. This doesn't
mean going to school on every occasion anything
happens, but let the teachers know about serious
worries and tell professionals your views – and
your child's.

Helping your child

Most of what you can do for your
child applies to all children. But if
your child has learning
difficulties, it is particularly
important to:

✔ spend time with him or her,
talking and listening

✔ pay attention to what your
child says and does

✔ involve him or her in making
decisions

✔ have high but realistic
aspirations

✔ be patient

Be fair on your child

You may find your child is frustratingly slow and doesn't grasp ideas you think are very easy – or that were learnt yesterday! Most children with learning difficulties do want to learn, but some find it a struggle. Hard as it is to avoid doing when frustration gets the better of you, it doesn't help to shout at or get very anxious with your child.

If we expect children to do badly, they usually do. Often we focus on what children with learning difficulties *can't* do. Concentrate on what your child *can* do and you'll be rewarded with your child's enthusiasm.

Parent quotes

"I make sure that I have some 'special' time with Alex every day – doing something together that we both enjoy. I think she benefits from knowing that she can talk to me during this time and have all of my attention."

"We were very worried that our child wasn't really progressing at school about four months ago. But he really seems to have knuckled down recently. We didn't have to do anything, I think he was just going through a bad patch."

We all tend to compare our child to other children. But try to remember that what really matters is how well your child is doing compared to his or her potential – and to how he or she was doing a few months ago or last year. How your child is progressing in the end matters more than where he or she is in the class.

Who can help?

You may find yourself dealing with a lot of different people and pieces of paper if your child is found to have learning difficulties – especially if he or she needs a statement or regular medical advice. A lot of people can help, depending on your child's needs. What is available and the titles that experts are given tend to change depending on where you live. So find out about these people and keep in touch with them.

AT YOUR CHILD'S SCHOOL, THERE WILL BE:

✔ your child's class teacher who knows him or her well, but is often with your child for only one or two years

✔ the school SENCO who ensures that records are kept and links the work of everyone in school

✔ the headteacher whom you can approach especially if you feel that other people are not getting it right

AND THERE MAY BE:

✔ other teachers at the school with specific time or expertise

✔ learning support assistants, especially where your child needs regular help or physical support with learning

---

The role of the professional

Professionals supporting your child have three main types of task:

1 assessing your child's needs

2 assessing what the next steps should be

3 supporting your child

All these tasks are important and related, and different professionals may be more important in one aspect than another. The professionals who are supporting your child use the reviews throughout the year to decide what they should do to help your child.

FROM THE HEALTH SERVICE, PEOPLE WORKING WITH YOUR CHILD MIGHT INCLUDE:

✔ speech or occupational therapists

✔ consultants and specialist doctors. It is important that you keep the school up-to-date on any treatment that your child is receiving

✔ child guidance workers for children with emotional dfficulties

In addition, your GP may be involved, especially if there are physical problems.

THE LOCAL EDUCATION AUTHORITY EMPLOYS:

- educational psychologists
- advisory teachers and other professionals with very specialised knowledge in subjects like hearing or visual impairment or computing for children with learning difficulties.

Both educational psychologists and advisory teachers have specific training and experience gained from working in several schools. Their role is mainly advisory and in assessing your child, but they can also help and advise you and others involved. Often they will observe your child, do tests and then suggest what you can do to help. They will also recommend other people with particular expertise or special aids or computer programmes that might be useful.

If your child is at Stage 4 or 5, you will be told of a named LEA officer who handles the process of statements and reviews. This person is your point of contact with the LEA.

Educational psychologists

Educational psychologists are trained teachers who have completed extra training in how children learn. They are not psychiatrists. Seeing a psychologist does not mean your child has mental health problems. Their role is very important in co-ordinating everyone's views. A psychologist will usually talk with you about your child after each observation.

Other people who can help and guide you are:

✔ *specialist groups* – for all sorts of special needs – often formed by parents of children with needs similar to your child's. Some addresses are listed at the back of this book. These organisations can be very helpful in giving advice and support because of their detailed knowledge. Remember to listen to a whole range of advice. It is possible to get so tied up in your child's condition that you forget that the decisions will affect your child's future.

✔ *health visitors* – especially for young children – can advise you on specific health issues. Generally they have wide-ranging experience of children and their health and learning problems and can be a source of information.

✔ *named persons* are volunteers who can offer advice and help – especially on issues you don't understand or are worried about. They have usually been through similar experiences themselves. You can get a list of named persons from your LEA, although they work completely independently of it.

✔ *friends and other parents who have children similar to yours* may be able to help you feel confident about approaching the school. Often this kind of support is the most helpful. But be careful – don't add to your anxiety by moaning or comparing your children's problems. Remember to celebrate the good things.

✔ *parents or carers* should discuss how to help their child – not always easy if a relationship has broken down. Often grandparents or other relatives may be helpful because they may not be quite so closely involved and could have a clearer perspective.

It is valuable to approach other people for help. At times you are bound to feel confused about weighing up which are the best options for your child and worried about whether you are making the right decision. You, as a parent, usually know your child best of all, but talking things through with other people usually does help.

There is a lot of information to help you understand the issues – especially on physical conditions – from books, pamphlets and the Internet. Often the LEA or specialist groups mentioned at the back of this book are the best source for these.

Parent quote

"We went out to get as much advice and information as possible. It seemed like we'd heard thousands of professional opinions, but it was worth it because the information gave us the confidence to make a solid decision."

Almost always, what you think is unique to your child has been faced by thousands of other people.

Work in partnership with the educational professionals to agree the best for your child.

Remember that other people usually want to help your child. Sometimes they are busy, or are short of resources and money, so you may need to remind them or stand up for your child's rights. Don't be afraid to do so, but do try to work with them and discuss your concerns and suggestions with them. Constant argument is time consuming and distressing. Do your best to agree if you can.

Emotional and behavioural problems

What should I do if my child has emotional or behavioural problems?

Most children at times behave badly and have emotional difficulties. Like some adults!

But **emotional and behavioural disturbance (EBD)** means more than slight unhappiness or naughtiness. Often children go through phases, but you should be concerned if your child shows signs of persistent or intense unhappiness and consistently defies rules and authority. This is often closely related to difficulty in learning – especially for boys.

Watch out for signs of unhappiness (such as bad dreams, withdrawn behaviour or tantrums) especially if they are not part of a usual pattern. The causes may be at home, such as jealousy of a new baby, bereavement or divorce. Or they may be at school, for instance bullying. Often situations such as these will affect your child's learning and if not dealt with may result in long-term unhappiness.

Don't get too anxious if your child seems to behave differently for a while, but watch for what happens over time. If the odd behaviour continues, talk to your child's teacher or doctor. Sometimes children do show signs of real disturbance, for instance by threatening their own or other people's safety. If you are really worried about your own, or your child's, safety, seek help straight away. Your GP can help with a referral to child guidance or other support.

Behavioural problems, especially when they occur outside the family unit, can lead to trouble at school. Children often get mixed up with others involved in bullying or crime. Keep an eye on the children your child befriends, especially if they are much older. If the school reports poor behaviour, take it seriously. Be firm if your child is getting into trouble, but try to understand what worries and fears may be causing the behaviour.

The best ways to help your child feel good about him or herself

✔ show interest in things that matter to your child

✔ provide security and firm boundaries

✔ have clearly understood expectations

What if my child defies me?

Make sure you have consistent but reasonable expectations of your child – about bedtimes, the amount of TV he or she can watch, when homework is to be done and sharing family meals. Your child may grumble, but these provide an important framework. Be firm. Giving in the whole time may seem easy, but if your child gets his or her way all the time it can cause all sorts of problems in the future.

Don't nag about things that don't really matter.

What if my child can't concentrate?

Most of us think our children are not good at paying attention. Parents have always thought that about children! But children can often concentrate for long periods – look at any young child totally absorbed in a puzzle or game, or an older child that you cannot drag away from playing computer games.

If your child is very able, his or her concentration may be very good or very bad. Poor concentration can be the result of boredom and sometimes it is worth setting – and helping with – challenges or projects to work at in addition to schoolwork. But be careful! Often, clever children try to get away with as much as possible and need boundaries and firm handling, just like other children.

CHILDREN ARE OFTEN BAD AT:

- persisting with tasks they don't really enjoy

- settling into routines when they have lots of choices

SO:

- be firm to ensure that your child settles down and finishes off what needs to be done

- use reward rather than punishment, whenever you can

- try to give extra care and attention, especially if you know your child is having a hard time

Attention deficit and hyperactivity disorder (ADHD)

You may have heard about **attention deficit and hyperactivity disorder (ADHD)**. This does not have the same effect as when a child cannot concentrate well. It is where children cannot concentrate for any length of time, and it is usually associated with disruptive behaviour. It is much more common in boys than girls. ADHD has to be diagnosed by a doctor or a psychologist who may recommend using a drug such as Ritalin. Do not immediately think your child has ADHD just because he or she finds it hard to concentrate; usually behavioural difficulties can be solved by giving firm boundaries for what is acceptable behaviour.

Learning difficulties in boys and girls

Boys and girls can both have emotional and behavioural difficulties, but the signs tend to be rather different. Boys will often be more aggressive and disruptive, and try to get far more attention. Girls will often be more withdrawn.

Some conditions, such as autism, are more common in boys. Eating disorders are more common in girls, but these are rarely serious until the secondary years.

Low achievement in boys

Behavioural difficulties in boys are often linked with low levels of achievement, especially in reading. Often children who find reading hard feel they are

no good at anything. This may lead to low self-esteem or the child giving up or resorting to bad behaviour. If children are not helped by the time they are seven or eight years old, they can easily get into a spiral of failure. It is vital to work hard to get children over this hurdle.

> **Parent quote**
>
> "My lad never could settle at school, he was always getting into trouble and so on. He got by at primary school but he really needed sorting out before he went on to the big school."

Don't panic!

Reading this book may make you think your child has all sorts of problems. Most children go through phases and at some point show signs to concern us. But with firmness and care most grow up to be happy, well-adjusted adults.

Watch out for signs of unhappiness in your child.

Problems with reading

How can I help my child with reading difficulties?

Learning to read is very important. Children who find reading hard often find other subjects difficult and have low self-esteem. Parents and teachers spend a lot of time and energy helping children who are struggling with reading.

There is never one moment when children can read – it is a gradual process. Some children start recognising words at the age of three, others not until they are five. Many go to school reading well, others hardly at all. Don't worry or feel that you have failed your pre-school child if you haven't taught him or her to read by the time he or she goes to school. But read together whenever you have the chance!

Is there any one effective way of teaching reading?

That's easy! No.

There is a lot of discussion about whether children should learn to read by whole words (**Look and Say**) or by sounding out letters (**Phonics**). The **Literacy Hour** stresses phonics a lot. Phonics doesn't work with some words, but can be very useful for unfamiliar words and for those struggling with reading. Look and Say works well for 'little' words and later on when a child is fluent. Some children seem to learn better with one way than the other – it is important to help them try to make use of both. Good readers usually learn through a variety of methods.

A few 'don'ts'

When helping your child with reading difficulties don't:

✗ just focus on reading – get your child to play word games such as 'I Spy' too

✗ give your child a hard time and put him or her off reading

✗ pass on your anxiety to your child if you can help it

✗ take your child's difficulties personally

When should I start to be worried if my child isn't doing well?

Observe your child's progress from a young age. If you think his or her language is weak, or he or she has speech difficulties, get help. A speech therapist may be able to find very simple ways of helping your child.

Boys generally find learning and using language harder than girls do. Of course, many boys do very well and some girls find reading difficult. But overall boys have more difficulties.

Keep on doing all the things that help children to learn about language – reading and telling stories to them; asking and answering questions; doing interesting activities; playing with them. Don't underestimate how vital this is – especially if you both enjoy it!

Most children have started to read by the time they are five. If your child hasn't, talk with the teacher. As a very broad rule of thumb, be concerned if your child gets to six years old without starting to read a few words. If your child is not 'on the way' by his or her seventh birthday, a plan of support should certainly be in place both at home and in the classroom.

What if my child is learning English as an additional language?

Children need to be confident speaking and listening to a language before reading it. If your child is learning English as an additional language, progress in reading and writing will probably be slower at first. He or she will probably score lower in tests and assessments. It is not that your child is stupid, or has special educational needs – he or she is simply taking longer to learn these skills. Many children with English as an additional language make the most progress with reading at the age of seven or eight, rather than five or six. Most children have caught up by the time they are about 11. When they leave school, many do much better than children with English as a first language.

Teachers, or other children, may think that children learning an additional language are of low ability. If this is the case there are several things you can do.

- Talk with teachers about your child's abilities both in English and the home language and be sure they understand your child's situation.
- Continue to work with your child to help him or her become fluent in spoken English.
- Always encourage and praise your child.

Be careful, though. It is possible that your child does have a learning difficulty like many others. Do not leave it too long before discussing this with teachers, especially if your child's language development in the home language is slow too.

What is dyslexia? Can I do anything about it?

There is fierce disagreement about **dyslexia** among educational professionals. Most professionals agree that some children have specific difficulties processing language. They see words jumbled up, or in a different order. This is called dyslexia, word-blindness or specific learning difficulties. Children who suffer from dyslexia find learning to read very difficult and frustrating and often writing is even harder.

THE TWO APPROACHES:

- ✔ some people believe that dyslexia is quite widespread and needs very specific and structured programmes (taking up a lot of time and resources)

- ✔ others think that only a few children really have dyslexia and that many children just have a period of difficulty which they will overcome naturally

Parent quote

"However much we practised, he never seemed to remember the words. In the end, we had him assessed and found he had dyslexia."

Is your child dyslexic?

If your child finds recognising and remembering words very difficult and doesn't read as quickly as other children, don't jump straight to the conclusion that he or she is dyslexic.

Discuss with teachers whether your child:

- ✔ is just slow getting started

- ✔ has particular difficulties and needs a special programme

Work with your child's teacher. If you agree to help every day for ten minutes, try to keep it up. If you have a home-school diary, fill it in. If you are concentrating on just a few key words, really work on them. You may not succeed straight away, but your child will benefit from regular and sympathetic support.

Keep working with your child. If progress is still slow and you are concerned, be more forceful when you talk to your child's teacher. Insist on an assessment.

Parent quote

"The home-school diary helped us to know what the teacher was doing so we could fit our help in around that."

Being diagnosed as dyslexic can be a huge relief for children who have been persevering with reading but have not progressed.

Problems with numbers and other subjects

How important are maths and other subjects?

We tend to focus too much on difficulties in reading and writing and think that other subjects don't matter as much to a child with learning difficulties. But maths and other subjects are important both in their own right and because success helps your child feel confident and interested. This is even more important if your child finds learning difficult.

Children need a wide range of experiences. Many children who find literacy hard do well in **other subjects**.

Success in one area often leads to confidence and success in others.

Are particular groups of children good at certain subjects?

Parent quote

"I was never much good at maths, so we didn't do so much of that with her as we did reading."

Be careful about making assumptions and stereotypes. You may hear that boys are better at practical activities, or that children with English as an additional language are good at maths and science. High expectations tend to lead to high achievement, so give your child the freedom to develop in any subject.

Focus on what your child does well rather than concentrating on problems. Encourage and help your child develop a wide range of abilities and interests – not just what you think or hope he or she should be good at.

What if I think I am no good at maths?

Many adults never really understood maths and are worried about it. Often people are afraid about anything to do with maths. They may feel suspicious about 'modern' maths, and be very unsure of what children of a certain age should be able to do.

Don't worry if you feel this way – you can still help just by encouraging your child and supporting him or her. Talking through maths problems and learning or finding out solutions together is a great way of helping and can be fun! And the greatest incentive for most children is you showing interest in the work your child is doing – you don't need a maths degree for that!

What is maths about?

Maths is not just about 'doing sums'. Important maths skills include:

- ✔ estimating and guessing

- ✔ looking for patterns and shapes

- ✔ working out how to resolve 'real life' calculations, such as working out the cost of something in a sale with a 50% reduction

- ✔ using mathematical words and terms such as bigger/smaller, longest/shortest, fractions and money

We use these skills in drawing, shopping, cooking, making models, and countless other everyday activities.

Remember that maths is:

- ✔ fun when well-presented and related to real life

- ✔ confusing if different people tell you different methods – so work with the teachers to teach your child consistently

How can I help with maths?

✔ make use of everyday situations, such as laying the table, to count things

✔ talk about shapes of road signs, compare the size of buildings or people

✔ play board games (such as snakes and ladders or Monopoly) or card games (such as Snap and pairs)

✔ look out for numbers, patterns and shapes in everyday situations

✔ use computer programmes if you have a computer

What about tests and multiplication tables?

Don't keep testing your child's maths – at least not formally. This may make him or her more anxious. Help with homework and preparing for tests – but make it enjoyable.

But do help your child learn multiplication tables when they are being taught at school. It will be useful, but not if your child is too young, nor if they are just learnt parrot-fashion. It is better to give your child problems to solve and make sure he or she understands what tables are all about. Start with the x2, x5 and x10 tables and don't move on to x7, x8 and x9 tables before your child is ready.

Can I help with science?

Science is about understanding the world around us. It is not just about Bunsen burners and chemicals! Many children with learning difficulties find reading and writing frustrating, so practical activities may inspire them and help them to succeed. Discuss things that happen in the world around – from blown fuses to boiling water, from the changing seasons to environmental issues. Encourage your child to ask questions. Answer if you can and don't be afraid to say you don't know. Why not find out together?

Do history and geography matter?

You may think that these are not so relevant for young children. But getting a sense of time and what happened in the past, as well as of the local community and the wider world, are important. Speaking to grandparents about the past, watching the TV, thinking about different routes to get to a friend's house – all these activities and many others help children to understand history and geography and feel more a part of the community.

Range of skills

Remember, learning is not just about reading and writing. Getting a broad range of different skills and developing wide interests may be more important in life than traditional subjects. Everyone has many different sorts of 'intelligence'.

All children with learning difficulties have a right to the full range of subjects – and can benefit from less traditional subjects as much as, or more than, those who find everything easy.

What is the importance of art and music?

If your child has learning difficulties, music and art are particularly important. They really help to build confidence. Many children who find reading and writing difficult have real aptitude for drawing and modelling; for listening to or composing music and for acting and imaginative play. Look out for chances to involve your child – especially in out-of-school clubs.

Are P.E. and drama anything more than just playing?

If your child has learning difficulties, he or she may find a lot of pleasure and fulfilment in physical activity – it allows children to use up some of their energy. Many children with learning difficulties excel – and build their confidence – in these areas. Children with physical disabilities may particularly enjoy and benefit from individual or small-group activities such as drama and swimming.

How can I help my child with physical difficulties?

Each child is an individual whose needs require individual assessment. This chapter cannot possibly discuss every child's difficulties. The term 'physical disabilities' covers a very wide range of needs – some permanent (from brain damage to slight hearing impairment), some temporary (from poor co-ordination to conditions requiring hospital care).

Some physical difficulties, such as impaired hearing, Down's syndrome or cystic fibrosis, require medical support from when your child is a baby. Some result in learning difficulties, but this is not always the case. Many children with physical disabilities do very well at school.

Even the physical difficulties that are less obvious or only temporary can make a big difference to a child's schooling. For example, many children suffer from slight hearing loss, perhaps caused by glue ear or frequent colds, and this can make classroom learning very difficult. Or some children find gripping a pencil difficult or may have **dyspraxia** (poor co-ordination). Physical difficulties such as these require a teacher to pay extra attention to the child, so in all cases you must keep the teacher informed of any physical difficulties your child has.

Special schools or mainstream schools?

A special school or unit may be best for some children with complicated or severe medical conditions. But many children with physical disabilities get on well in mainstream schools, especially in the primary years. Children with severe medical needs, especially following a major operation, may require a hospital school.

Children should be educated in the school that suits their needs best, if necessary with adaptations and support.

Parent quote

"We had to ask, but I was really surprised that the council agreed to pay for a special computer for him because his eyesight was so bad."

Can I get someone to help my child with specific exercises?

This depends on your child's disability. Schools don't always have the necessary resources. They will usually try to help if it does not mean employing someone extra. You will need to approach your LEA about extra resources, but you might need to press them to provide what your child needs. Your GP may well support you in your requests.

Often a few minutes a day spent on cutting and sticking, stretching specific muscles, or bouncing a ball can help children improve poor co-ordination or overcome other physical difficulties. These are things that you can just as easily do at home with your child as in school.

> **What is integration?**
>
> Integration means educating children with disabilities in schools alongside other children. This has worked very well for many children – especially those with a physical disability. It has been less successful in other cases, especially where extra support has been inadequate.

What if my child needs medication?

This is tricky. In special schools, someone will often be available to give your child his or her drugs. Mainstream schools may not have anyone able to administer medication. Most will help if it does not involve injections or skilled intervention. If so, you may need to make specific arrangements. But attitudes vary, so discuss this with the headteacher in advance.

So which is the best school for my child?

There is no simple answer. In the early years many children with considerable disabilities do well at the local primary school. But this may change as children get older. Often resources become a real issue. You need both to stand up for what you think is best for your child and to listen to the advice of professionals. Discussions and reviews are important and statements (usually needed before a special school is suggested) are crucial.

WHEN CONSIDERING YOUR CHILD'S NEEDS:

- ✔ contact the LEA to get a statement outlining your child's needs

- ✔ tell your child's teacher about previous and current physical difficulties and pass on records

- ✔ have your child's eyesight and hearing tested if you have concerns about either

- ✔ be prepared to say if you think your child's needs are not being recognised or met

> **Parent quote**
>
> "I couldn't have asked for more. She was made so welcome at the local school, though later on she had to go to the special school."

So what can I do to make schooling easier for my child?

✔ Watch out for what helps your child and tell professionals about it.

✔ Look out for changes in your child, which only you may notice.

✔ Find out about your child's condition and let others know – especially if it is rare. Remember many organisations help parents in this situation – some are mentioned at the end of this book

✔ Talk with doctors, nurses and the school's headteacher well before your child starts school or nursery, especially if adaptations or extra help may be needed.

Don't assume that everyone else knows what is obvious to you. You know your child better, and spend more time with him or her, than anyone. Be prepared to be assertive but also to listen to other people who may have worked with similar children many times before. Doctors, teachers and others are often busy and the powers-that-be listen to parents much more than to children. So press for speech therapy, or extra help, or a special toilet – whatever your child needs.

Be prepared to say if you think your child's needs are not being recognised or met.

Should I worry about bullying?

Your child may get bullied at school. Or he or she may be a bully. Bullying is different from arguments or fights. It can mean name calling (often about family, race or looks), teasing, ganging up or hurting other children.

Bullying takes place repeatedly and is deliberately unkind or hurtful, and almost always between people who aren't friends. The bully is exerting power over someone weaker. Bullying can affect boys and girls of all ages. It can lead to serious unhappiness, problems with learning and even crime if it continues.

If your child complains about bullying, ask what he or she means. A dispute or argument between friends is probably not bullying.

Parent tip

"Do not assume that your child is always telling the truth! Try to find out how the whole incident started before laying the blame anywhere."

So what should you do if your child is being bullied?

✔ help your child to be independent and assertive

✔ encourage your child to talk about problems

✔ if you are worried about your child, listen and watch him or her to discover the reason for the unhappiness

✔ ask what the problem is without interrogating your child

Even when you ask, your child may not say when he or she is being bullied, in case the bullying gets worse.

Some children are particularly vulnerable to being bullied. Sometimes they are physically small or children who are loners or 'different'; sometimes it is those who are very able or those with slight speech or language impediments. But all children may be bullied – so watch out for the signs.

Stop bullying

Everyone – especially children being bullied – wants bullying to stop. We are all responsible for ensuring that this happens by:

✔ showing children ways to deal with it, or not get involved in it

✔ intervening ourselves when and if it gets more serious

If bullying continues:

✔ don't confront the bully yourself. It may make things worse

✔ talk with your child and with teachers. Agree on who does what

✔ be there to help but try not to interfere all the time

✔ keep checking to see if things improve

Don't tell your child to fight back – this will be against the school rules and will get your child into trouble. It may even lead to your child becoming a bully later in life.

Help your child to see that the bullying must stop

Most bullies and victims of bullies are boys. Because when boys bully they often cause fights or violence, schools notice it more. But girls tend to bully and be bullied in different ways – more quietly and subtly, through words and excluding other children from friendship groups. It can be harder to spot and to deal with, but can cause real distress.

Children who are black or from ethnic minorities frequently suffer bullying. Children often – like adults – find people who are different threatening, and can be very hurtful, especially with name calling. Sadly, schools sometimes dismiss it as playful. Your child should not have to cope with it. It can lead to serious harassment and problems later on in life. Let the school know and be assertive in asking them to deal with it. The school will probably have a policy to deal with bullying. If not, speak to the headteacher or a governor and ask to have one put in place.

Discuss with your child how to react towards bullies. Repeat what you discuss, or write it down for your child to remember. This advice might include:

- ✔ ignoring taunts for a while, especially if your child is easily provoked

- ✔ walking away with a friend

- ✔ playing a particular game with other people, especially at playtimes

- ✔ saying 'Stop it! I don't like being called names!'

- ✔ telling a dinner lady or a teacher and, importantly, telling someone else if that doesn't work

- ✔ going to speak to the deputy head or headteacher if need be

Some young children find break or dinner time difficult, especially at a new school. Schools want to – and can – help but don't always know what is happening. When bullying happens in the playground, teachers may not notice straight away.

Bullying often occurs on the way to or from school, when children walk on their own, or on the school bus. This is hard for schools to deal with – but they usually want to help, maybe by informing the other child's parents. If your child is suffering in this way, the answer may be simply to arrange for your child to go home with an adult or a group of friends every day. Your child may resent the loss of independence, but insist – your role is to keep him or her safe and your child will probably be grateful when the problem is resolved.

WHAT IF MY CHILD IS A BULLY?

As a parent you will naturally, and rightly, always want to take your child's side. But remember there is another side – your child may not always tell the whole truth. It may actually be your child that is a bully. If so try to stop him or her by:

- ✔ trying to understand why your child may feel the need to bully

- ✔ expressing your disapproval and by appropriate punishment. This often involves an apology face to face – with an adult present – to the bully's victim or in writing

- ✔ explaining the impact that the bullying is having on the other child, and reminding your child of times when he or she was bullied

- ✔ supporting the school in how it decides to treat the situation

- ✔ checking up later on with the school that it has stopped

Sometimes the cause may be more deep-seated and you may wish to seek professional guidance through your GP.

Girls and bullying

Do not assume that girls never have problems with their emotions and behaviour.

Sometimes bullying among girls can be subtle and unpleasant.

Watch out for withdrawn behaviour, especially when this is a change from normal. This may be a sign that your child is being bullied.

What are my rights and responsibilities?

Always remember that all children are different. If your child has a slight learning delay or a temporary problem, you will not encounter many of the issues covered in this book.

If your child has complicated learning difficulties or a permanent medical condition, you will need a lot of information in addition to what is in this book. You may find yourself dealing with a lot of different people and mountains of paperwork, especially if your child needs a statement. Informing yourself about what is going on is the best way of coping.

Being a parent is hard work. You have both rights over your child and responsibilities for him or her. Some are set down in law, but mostly helping your child is down to using common sense and keeping things in perspective.

Talking with teachers and other professionals helps parents of a child with learning difficulties plan what to do next. So the reviews during the different stages of your child's development are really important. But remember, professionals are often working under pressure. You need to remind them of your child's needs.

You have a right to:

4 full, regular and accurate information from your child's school

✔ involvement in the identification and assessment of your child, including regular reviews

✔ your views being fully considered when decisions about your child are made, such as on adaptations to buildings or which school your child should be at

In addition, you have many legal rights, such as rights of appeal and tribunals, especially if you disagree with what is suggested. Don't be afraid to exercise them if you really feel your views have not been considered. This should be seen as a last resort. Think carefully whether all the trouble and hassle is going to be worth it, because this can be distressing for both your child and you.

When do professionals have to intervene?

Professionals have legal responsibilities. One that can be very hard for you as a parent relates to child protection. If a teacher, or doctor, thinks that your child may be suffering abuse, he or she has to report it. This abuse may be:

✔ physical, if your child shows signs of being hit or hurt

✔ emotional, if your child seems to be neglected or uncared-for

✔ sexual, if someone may have interfered with him or her

The suspicion may be unfounded, and may have nothing to do with you. But children have to be protected. If you need help to keep your child safe, talk to the social services who will help as much as they can.

Before a meeting with an educational specialist:

✔ plan what you want to say

✔ take a friend (or a named person), someone you really trust, especially for meetings you think will be difficult or if you are not confident in English or find reading difficult

✔ keep notes of meetings and who has agreed to do what

What are my responsibilities?

You have many responsibilities towards your child.
These include:

1 keeping your child safe

2 helping your child do well

3 seeing that your child's needs are met as fully as possible

4 contributing honestly and fully to assessments and decisions

5 working in partnership with professionals when you can

It is important that you keep the school informed about consultants' advice or health problems, about domestic difficulties or how your child is at home. Where confidentiality is an issue, make sure that professionals know what you want to be kept private.

Parent quote

"My friend had a child who'd had the same problem. Having her along at the meeting was a real help because she could say things that I wasn't too sure about."

This book is about learning difficulties. Inevitably it has concentrated on possible problems. But remember that all children bring pleasure and frustration to their parents. Children with learning difficulties are no different. Sometimes they disappoint us, usually they give us great joy. Remember that your child needs to:

✔ be protected and cared for

✔ grow up into an independent adult

Do not expect him or her to be just like you or to fit in with all your hopes. Give your child love, care and support – these are the soundest base for learning and life that a child can have.

> **Parent quote**
>
> "I never thought she would, but in the end she left primary school really confident and able to stand up for herself."

Work with your child to overcome his or her learning difficulties.

Glossary

Attainment Targets   Targets for children's learning in each subject at different stages. Each attainment target is divided into eight levels, like steps up a ladder.

Attention deficit and hyperactivity disorder (ADHD)   A medical condition, diagnosed by a doctor, where children cannot concentrate for any length of time, usually associated with disruptive behaviour. Much more specific than 'being a naughty boy' – but much more common in boys than girls.

Baseline Assessment   Teacher observation of children within the first seven weeks of entering the Reception class, which is used to assess learning levels in maths, English and social skills.

Code of Practice   The government guidance setting out the various responsibilities of schools, LEAs and others in relation to special educational needs (SEN).

Core subjects   The main subjects in the National Curriculum: English, maths and science. R.E. (religious education) and I.C.T. (Information and Communications Technology) are also treated like core subjects. These are the only subjects where set Programmes of Study have to be taught in full.

Dyslexia   A difficulty with processing written language, usually leading to quite severe problems with reading and writing. The causes of dyslexia and which children to include in the category lead to a lot of disagreement. Sometimes called word-blindness or 'specific learning difficulties' though this also covers other conditions.

Dyspraxia   A difficulty with physical actions and co-ordination.

Educational psychologist   A specialist employed by the Local Education Authority to assess children with SEN and advise schools and parents.

Emotional and behavioural disturbance (EBD)   A term covering children who have special needs related to emotional upset or behaviour difficulties.

English as an additional language   The term used where a child's first language is not English. Not a reason, as such, for children to be on the register of SEN, though of course some will be for other reasons.

Foundation subjects   Subjects covered in schools as part of the National Curriculum which are not English, maths and science (the core subjects) or R.E. and I.C.T. These include history, geography, music, design technology, art and P.E.

Individual Education Plan (IEP) A summary of the provision and targets the school sets for a pupil with SEN on Stage 2 or above.

Information and Communications Technology (I.C.T.) The term to replace I.T. (Information Technology) meaning the use of computers and other electronic means to enhance learning.

Integration The word used when children with learning difficulties attend a school where the whole range of ability is included.

Key Stages Stages at which a child's education can be assessed, after following a programme of work. There are four Key Stages, dividing ages 5-7, 7-11, 11-14 and 14-16.

Literacy Hour The time each day which schools have to devote to teaching literacy skills.

Local Education Authority (LEA) The county, borough or district education authority. LEAs have many specific roles especially in admissions, finance and special educational needs.

Look and Say Teaching or learning reading by looking at the shape of the whole word or part of it, rather than breaking it into sounds.

Mainstream schools The sort of schools which the majority of children attend. Most children with SEN will also attend them, often getting extra help if need be.

Multi-professional assessment (MPA) The process at Stage 4 of the Code of Practice by which the LEA gathers the advice and views of teachers, the SENCO, a doctor, an educational psychologist and other professionals involved on what to do. Parents' views are very important in this.

Named persons Volunteers to advise and help parents especially when dealing with issues you don't understand or are worried about. LEAs keep a list of these people.

National Curriculum The government's system of education broken into four Key Stages, which applies to all pupils of compulsory school age in maintained schools. It contains core and foundation (non-core) subjects, and incorporates National Tests at the end of each Key Stage.

National Tests Formerly known as SATS, these tests are taken in school at the end of each Key Stage — at ages 7, 11 and 14 — to determine what Attainment Target pupils have reached. The scores are also used, especially at age 11, to compare the results of schools as a whole.

OFSTED (Office for Standards in Education) The government department which oversees inspections and sends teams to assess individual schools.

Phonics Teaching or learning reading based on the sounds of letters.

Reviews Formal meetings with teachers and other professionals to see how your child is progressing.

SEN   The abbreviation often used for special educational needs

Special needs co-ordinator (SENCO)
A senior teacher appointed by each school to oversee the provision in the school and advise other teachers.

Special needs register   The list of children with SEN identified by each school and maintained by the SENCO.

Special schools   Schools (usually day, but can be boarding) specially designed for children with learning, behavioural or physical difficulties. Almost always requiring a 'statement' for children to attend them, though many children with statements will attend mainstream schools or units.

Special unit   Usually a small building attached to but separate from a mainstream school catering for children with a particular difficulty (such as visual or hearing impairment) where children spend most of the time – but often enabling integration for part of the day or part of the week.

Statement   A document drawn up by the LEA to outline the provision it deems necessary to help children with considerable difficulties- and how it intends to meet their needs, almost always including resources. Parents get a copy and are invited to a review of the statement at least once a year.

Teacher assessment   The teacher's own judgements about the level of progress children have made. This is both a part of deciding what and how to teach, and also takes place more formally at set times, especially with the National Tests at 7, 11 and 14 years old.

USEFUL INFORMATION

Advisory Centre for Education (ACE)
Department A, Unit 1B, Aberdeen Studios,
22 Highbury Grove, London, N5 2DQ
Web: www.ace-ed.org.uk/
Phone: 020 7354 8321
Free advice, information and support for parents
of children in state schools

Basic Skills Agency
7th Floor, Commonwealth House
1-19 New Oxford Street, London
WC1A 1NU
Web: www.basic-skills.co.uk/
Phone: 020 7405 4017
National development agency for basic literacy
and numeracy skills

British Dyslexia Association
98 London Road, Reading RG1 5AU
Web: www.bda-dyslexia.org.uk
Phone: 0118 966 8271
Fax: 0118 935 1927
Email: info@dyselxiahelp-bda.demon.co.uk
Provides information on dyslexia and access to
local support groups.

DfEE (Department for Education and Employment)
Sanctuary Buildings, Great Smith Street,
London SW1P 3BT
Web: www.dfee.gov.uk
Phone: 020 7925 5000
Free publications on all aspects of education can
be sent out, available by phoning 01787 880 946
The website for special needs is
www.dfee.gov.uk/sen

Education Extra
St Margaret's House, 17 Old Ford Road,
London, E2 9DL
Web: www.educationextra.org.uk
Phone: 020 8983 1061
Useful advice for parents on different aspects of
education.

MENCAP (Royal Society for the Mentally Handicapped)
123 Golden Lane, London EC1Y 0RT
Web: www.mencap.org.uk
Phone: 020 7454 0454
Fax: 020 7608 3254
General information and publications list
available, as well as local contacts.

National Association for Gifted Children
Elder House, Milton Keynes MK9 1LR
Web: www.rmplc.co.uk/orgs/nagc
Phone: 01908 673 677
Fax: 01908 673 679
Email nagc@rmplc.co.uk
Provides support groups for counselling for
parents and children. Branches throughout UK.
Information leaflets available.

National Association for Special Educational Needs
NASEN House, 4/5 Amber Business Village,
Amber Close, Amington, Tamworth, B77 4RP
Web: www.nasen.org.uk
Phone: 01827 311 500

National Confederation for Parent Teacher Associations (NCPTA)
2 Ebbsfleet Estate, Stonebridge Road, Gravesend
Kent DA11 9DZ
Web: www.rmplc.co.uk/orgs/ncpta
Phone: 01474 560 618
Promotes partnership between home and
school, children, parents, teachers and education
authorities.

REACH (National Research Centre for Children with Reading Difficulties)
California Country Park, Nine Mile Ride,
Finshampstead, Berkshire RG40 4HT
Web: www.reach-reading.demon.co.uk
Phone: 0118 973 7575
Fax: 0118 973 7105
For anyone caring for a child with a disability,
illness or learning problem which affects their
reading, language or communication.

Royal National Institute for the Blind
224-228 Great Portland Street
London W1N 6AA
Web: www.rnib.org.uk
Phone: 020 7388 1266
Fax: 020 7383 4921
Publications and leaflets for those working with
people with visual and learning difficulties, with
an Education Information Service.

WEBSITES

www.hometown.aol.com/wiseowlsw
A UK children's specialist in education software
to play online or download

www.bbc.co.uk/education/schools/
primary.shtml
Home and school learning resources for
children. The BBC education site as a whole has
resources to cover a large range of educational
issues.